Animals Small and Huge

CONTENTS

NATIONAL GEOGRAPHIC Hampton-Brown

School Publishing

Words with Soft c

Look at each picture. Read the words.

ce
ci_

Example:

cent

mi**ce**

fa**ce**

pri**ce** $3.50

la**ce**

sli**ce** of cake

ri**ce**

High Frequency
Words

| eyes |
| far |
| small |
| three |
| through |
| under |

Key Words

Look at the picture.

Read the sentences.

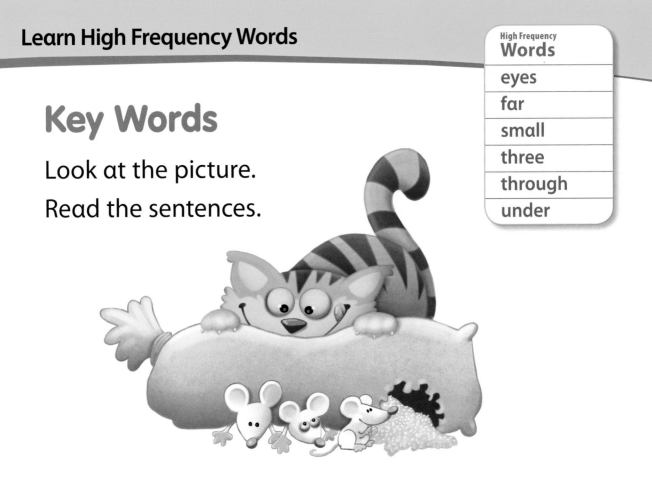

Mice Find Food

1. **Three** **small** mice eat rice **through** a hole.
2. Then they see a cat's big **eyes**!
3. The mice hide **under** the bag.
4. The mice are not **far** from the cat.

What will the three mice do next?

Phonics Games

NGReach.com

3

Many Kinds of Mice

by Deanne W. Kells

There are many kinds of mice.

The mice are not all the same.

1 field mice

2 deer mice

3 jumping mice

We will look at three kinds of mice.

city

maze

field

Field Mice

These mice live in fields far from the city. They like a lot of space! The mice make mazes through the field. They race through the mazes.

log

These mice are small. They have small faces and eyes. They sleep under logs or rocks.

Deer Mice

These mice live in nests under logs.

You will not see a trace of them.

deer mice

These mice are tan and white. Their faces look like deer faces. They have eyes twice as big as field mice!

deer

grass

Jumping Mice

Jumping mice live in places with grass.
They use grass to make their nests.

long back leg

These small mice have long back legs for jumping. They can jump quite far from place to place.

Which mice do you like best?

Can it be nice to have mice as pets? ❖

Words with Soft c

Read these words.

rice	maze	eat	race
space	trace	slice	fit

Find the words with soft **c**.
Use letters to build them.

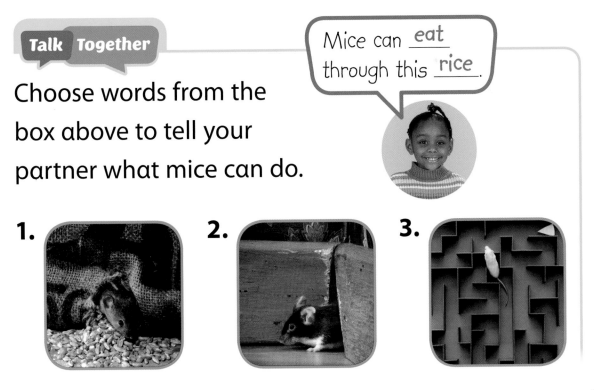

Talk Together

Choose words from the box above to tell your partner what mice can do.

Mice can __eat__ through this __rice__.

1.

2.

3.

Words with Soft <u>g</u>

Look at each picture. Read the words.

ge
gi_
_dge

Example:

<u>**ge**</u>m

pa<u>**ge**</u>

sta<u>**ge**</u>

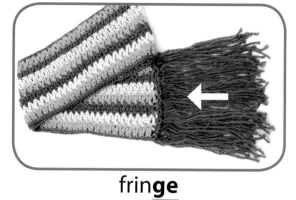

frin<u>**ge**</u>

bri<u>**dge**</u>

he<u>**dge**</u>

Key Words

Read the sentences. Match each sentence to one of the pictures.

1. **2.** **3.**

One, Two, Three Giraffes

1. One giraffe stands **under** a tree.
2. A mother keeps her **eyes** on her **small** baby.
3. The mother does not let the baby go **far**.
4. **Three** giraffes walk **through** the trees.

How many small giraffes do you see?

Phonics Games
NGReach.com

15

Giraffes

by Kelsey Bruce

What do giraffes look like? Giraffes
are big!

You can stand up under them. Each
hoof is huge. It is the size of a plate.

eye

lashes

lips

Giraffes have big eyes. They can see far. Look at that thick fringe of lashes! Giraffes have thick lips as well. Branches and twigs do not poke their lips.

Why does a giraffe have spots? The
spots are not strange. They help it hide.
The spots look like sun and shade.

leaves

What do giraffes eat? They like leaves best. A big giraffe will walk through a wide range to find leaves. It must eat a lot of leaves to get full!

legs

lake

How do giraffes drink? They go to the edge of a lake. They must stretch their legs so wide!

walking giraffe

running giraffe

How do giraffes use their legs? They walk or run. But they change how they use their legs.

resting giraffe

How do giraffes rest? They rest a lot.
But they may not close their eyes.

lips

neck

leg

hoof

a giraffe's body

Giraffes start out small. They walk, run, sleep, eat, and drink. Then they grow up to be huge! What is the best thing a giraffe's body has? You be the judge. ❖

Words with Soft g

Read these words.

gem	jumped	bridge	crossed
cage	tire	changed	hedge

Find the words with soft **g**.
Use letters to build them.

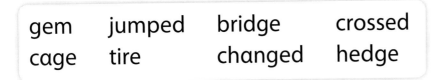

Talk Together

Choose words from the box above to tell your partner how the man got to the giraffe.

The man ___crossed___ a ___bridge___.

X
start

25

What Is It?

Look at the pictures with a partner. Take turns reading the clues. Then name the animal.

 1 I walk far through a wide range of space.

 2 I am almost twice as big as this small truck.

 3 My small eyes look through a fringe of lashes.

4 I have a strange nose on my face.

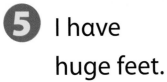

5 I have huge feet.

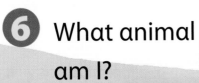

6 What animal am I?

Acknowledgments

Grateful acknowledgment is given to the authors, artists, photographers, museums, publishers, and agents for permission to reprint copyrighted material. Every effort has been made to secure the appropriate permission. If any omissions have been made or if corrections are required, please contact the Publisher.

Photographic Credits

CVR (Cover) Keren Su/Digital Vision/Getty Images. **2** (bl) Yue Tong Law/iStockphoto. (br) ZTS/ Shutterstock. (cl) Digital Vision/Getty Images. (cr) GaryAlvis/iStockphoto. (tl) Skip Odonnell/ iStockphoto. (tr) Vassiliy Vishnevskiy/iStockphoto. **3** (b) Liz Garza Williams/Hampton-Brown/ National Geographic School Publishing. **4** Ulrike Schanz/Animals Animals. **5** (b) Morgan, C. Allan/National Geographic Image Collection. (tl) David Aubrey/Corbis. (tr) Joe McDonald/ Corbis. **6** (inset) Wildlife/Peter Arnold, Inc.. **6-7** (bg) George Green/iStockphoto. **7** (inset) Stephen Dalton/Minden Pictures. **8** Joe McDonald/Corbis. **9** (b) Karel Brož/Shutterstock. (t) Mc Donald Wildlife Photog./Animals Animals. **10-11** Bruce Dale/National Geographic Image Collection. **11** (inset) Joe McDonald/Corbis. **12** Juniors Bildarchiv/Alamy Images. **13** (c) Eric Isselée/Shutterstock. (l) Adrian Davies/Nature Picture Library. (r) Mike Kemp/Jupiterimages. (t) Liz Garza Williams/Hampton-Brown/National Geographic School Publishing. **14** (bl) Uwe Bumann/Shutterstock. (br) Dan Moore/iStockphoto. (cl) Inti St Clair/Digital Vision/Getty Images. (cr) Sasha Davas/Shutterstock. (tl) ryasick photography/Shutterstock. (tr) Susan Trigg/ iStockphoto. **15** (b) Liz Garza Williams/Hampton-Brown/National Geographic School Publishing. (tc) Abrahams/Shutterstock. (tl) Getty Images/Jupiterimages. (tr) Juergen & Christine Sohns/ Animals Animals. **16** Michelle Van Meter/iStockphoto. **17** (inset) Jim Tuten/Animals Animals. (t) Images of Africa Photobank/Alamy Images. **18** R.P.B/Shutterstock. **19** Martin Heigan. (bg) BORTEL Pavel/Shutterstock. **20** Anup Shah/Photodisc/Alamy Images. **21** Paul Goldstein/ Imagestate. **22** (l) Gerrit_de_Vries/Shutterstock. (r) ABPL/Gerald Hinde/Animals Animals. **23** Gabriela Staebler/Corbis. **24** John Weaver/National Geographic Image Collection. (inset) Digital Vision/Getty Images. **25** (t) Liz Garza Williams/Hampton-Brown/National Geographic School Publishing. **26** (br) Etienne Oosthuizen/Shutterstock. (cr) Warwick Lister-Kaye/ iStockphoto. (tr) Markus Divis/iStockphoto. **26-27** (bg) Markus Divis/iStockphoto. **27** (bl) Etienne Oosthuizen/Shutterstock. (br) Nico Smit/iStockphoto. (cl) Andy Nowack/iStockphoto. (cr) Miguel Malo/iStockphoto. (tl) Vera Volkova/Shutterstock. (tr) Deborah Benbrook/ Alamy Images.

Illustrator Credits

3 Peter Grosshauser. **25** Durga Bernhard.

The National Geographic Society

John M. Fahey, Jr., President & Chief Executive Officer
Gilbert M. Grosvenor, Chairman of the Board

National Geographic School Publishing
Hampton-Brown
www.NGSP.com

Printed in the USA.
RR Donnelley, Jefferson City, MO

ISBN: 978-0-7362-8038-9

12 13 14 15 16 17 18 19
10 9 8 7 6 5 4

New High Frequency Words

eyes
far
small
three
through
under

Target Sound/Spellings

Soft c	Soft g
Selection: **Many Kinds of Mice**	**Selection:** **Giraffes**
face(s)	change
mice	edge
nice	fringe
place(s)	huge
race	judge
space	range
trace	strange
twice	